The Principal Portfolio

The Principal Portfolio

Genevieve Brown
Beverly J. Irby

CORWIN PRESS, INC.
A Sage Publications Company
Thousand Oaks, California

For information:

 Corwin Press, Inc.
A Sage Publications Company
2455 Teller Road
Thousand Oaks, California 91320
E-mail: order@corwin.sagepub.com

SAGE Publications Ltd.
6 Bonhill Street
London EC2A 4PU
United Kingdom

SAGE Publications India Pvt. Ltd.
M-32 Market
Greater Kailash I
New Delhi 110 048 India

Printed in the United States of America

Library of Congress Cataloging-in-Publication Data

Brown, Genevieve.
The principal portfolio / Genevieve Brown, Beverly J. Irby.
    p.   cm.
Includes bibliographical references.
ISBN 0-8039-6541-9 (cloth : acid-free paper). — ISBN
0-8039-6542-7 (pbk. : acid-free paper)
    1. School principals—United States.   2. School principals—Rating
of—United States.   3. Portfolios in education—United States.
4. School improvement programs—United States.   I. Irby, Beverly J.
II. Title.
LB2831.92.B77   1997
371.2'012—dc21   97-4757

This book is printed on acid-free paper.

97 98 99 00 01 02 03   10 9 8 7 6 5 4 3 2 1

Production Editor: S. Marlene Head
Editorial Assistant: Kristen L. Green
Typesetter/Designer: Andrea D. Swanson
Cover Designer: Marcia R. Finlayson

Contents

Preface

When successful organizations are analyzed, the importance of the leader in establishing and articulating the vision, in molding the culture, and in facilitating change becomes obvious. School reform efforts have focused attention on the principal as the one who can facilitate the process of transforming schools and leading the faculty, staff, students, and community to levels of excellence.

The job of the principal is complex, multifaceted, and demanding, and the principal's responsibilities and roles are many. Studies of high-performing principals and effective schools have taught us that the role of the principal as the instructional leader is paramount. The principal must develop and sustain a community where learning is the number one priority. Principals have recognized that to transform schools, they themselves must become continuous learners. Joyce and Showers (1995) have pointed out that professional growth is essential to creating optimum learning conditions for student success. Principals must become more reflective and their practice must become more informed. New expectations of principals call for new ways of "doing business" and for new resources.

The Principal Portfolio is a resource that holds great potential. It provides authentic documentation of the complicated and situational work of principals on their campuses, and it promotes self-assessment and reflection essential for improving practice and transforming schools. The value of portfolios for teachers and students is widely acknowledged. Only recently have administrators begun to recognize the great potential the administrative portfolio holds for improving schools. The development and use of the principal portfolio is in an embryonic stage. Results thus far are not disappointing, however, and used thoughtfully and intentionally by the principal, the portfolio is fulfilling its promises. This book offers principals hands-on, practical information on how to develop and use the principal portfolio to improve their performance and to assist in transforming their schools.

Chapter 1 describes the concept of the principal portfolio and explains why it is needed. Chapter 2 provides an overview of what should be included in the principal portfolio. Chapter 3, on professional growth, presents the importance of reflection and explains specifically how to develop reflective practice. Chapter 4 focuses on the principal portfolio for evaluation. Chapter 5 specifies how to develop and use the principal portfolio in career advancement.

Certainly, the improvement of principal practice and the transformation of schools is complicated. The principal portfolio is neither a cure-all nor a quick fix. The portfolio development process is intensive; it requires much thought, time, and effort. In our work with principals in the development and use of portfolios, we have found that the portfolio is a powerful tool for promoting self-analysis and professional growth aimed at improved practice, which can positively affect student achievement.

About the Authors

Genevieve Brown is currently Professor, Director of Doctoral Studies, and Chair of the Department of Educational Leadership and Counseling at Sam Houston State University, Huntsville, Texas. She also serves as University Supervisor for principal interns. She has intensive experience as an administrator in public schools, including 10 years as assistant superintendent and superintendent. She is also a trained assessor in the National Association of Secondary School Principals' principal assessment model. Her research and writing, focused on leadership theory, administrative portfolio development, administrator career development, administrator evaluations, organizational structures, staff development, and equity issues, have been published in books and journals. She is coeditor of several books on leadership, including *Women as School Executives: A Powerful Paradigm*, *Women as School Executives: Voices and Visions*, and *Supervision and Site-Based Decision-Making: Roles, Relationships, Responsibilities, and Realities*. Additionally, she is co-principal investigator of several grants and has served on several state and national organizations' executive boards. She is a consultant to school districts and was recently named to the International Who's Who of Women. She was recognized in Texas as Outstanding Instructional

Leader, in addition to Outstanding Woman Educator, and was most recently awarded the Renaissance Group Research Fellow Award.

Beverly J. Irby is Associate Professor and Coordinator of Research for the Center of Research and Doctoral Studies in the Department of Educational Leadership and Counseling at Sam Houston State University. Additionally, at the university she has served as Director of Field Experiences, Supervisor of Mentor Services, Liaison for the Urban Professional Developmental Site, and as a Title VII Grant Coordinator on an urban elementary school campus. Before this, she was an elementary school principal, assistant superintendent, and superintendent of schools, as well as a school psychologist, educational diagnostician, and special education director. Her research, writing, and presentations have explored the principalship, administrative portfolio development, general and women's leadership issues, personnel and program evaluation, program development in bilingual education, parent involvement, gifted education, science education, and adolescent pregnancy and parenting programs. She is author or coauthor of numerous grants totaling $4 million and often serves as a consultant to school districts. A recent research grant was awarded to explore the uses of computerized portfolios for administrators. She is a member of the International Who's Who of Women and has received the Texas Council of Women School Educators' Outstanding Educator Award and the Renaissance Group Research Fellow Award. She is coeditor or coauthor of four books on women's issues, *Women as School Executives: A Powerful Paradigm*, *Women as School Executives: Voices and Visions*, *The Teen Pregnancy and Parenting Handbook*, and *The Discussion Guide: The Teen Pregnancy and Parenting Handbook*.

1

The Principal Portfolio: Why It's Needed

Since we began the process of implementing principal portfolios, specifically for evaluation purposes, we have seen several positive outcomes—one is that the dialogue between the principals and the central administrators has opened up. Another is that we see how this process has the potential to improve leadership among our principals and us and how that can positively affect students and teachers.

Assistant superintendent

In public and university classrooms, the value of portfolios for students and teachers is widely acknowledged. Recently, principals have begun to recognize the merits of portfolios and to use portfolios for professional growth, evaluation, and career advancement. Although portfolio use results in several positive outcomes, the major benefit for principals is that the self-assessment and reflection inherent in portfolio development promotes administrator growth, which leads to improved performance and, ultimately, to improved schools and learning. This chapter describes the principal portfolio, explains its three uses, and summarizes benefits of principal portfolios.

The principal portfolio, whether for the purposes of professional growth, evaluation, or career advancement, is a collection of thoughtfully selected exhibits or artifacts and reflections indicative of an individual's experiences and ability to lead and of the individual's progress toward and/or attainment of established goals or criteria. Portfolio development involves (a) the selection of relevant artifacts (carefully selected documents that reflect attainment of or progress toward established criteria); (b) the writing of a reflection that describes, analyzes, and assesses leadership experiences illustrated by the artifacts; and (c) a written plan for future actions based on assessment and analysis.

Portfolio Uses

The first use of the portfolio, to encourage professional growth, emphasizes self-assessment and analysis of behaviors as they relate to the principal's performance. Because the major purpose is to determine areas in need of improvement, the professional growth portfolio is primarily for personal use and may or may not be shared with others. The portfolio in this case serves as a "check point" not only for assessing progress but also for determining whether goals should be reconsidered or modified. Although the principal's progress toward established goals may be reviewed by others, as in a peer coaching or formative evaluation situation, no value judgment is placed on the progress. However, implied judgment may be imposed as to the degree of satisfaction the principal has with his or her own progress toward the established goals.

> I have a portfolio that I developed only for my professional growth. I don't worry too much about its appearance. I just keep several artifacts on various projects on which I am working. I have reflections there too. My reflections really help me to grow in my leadership skills and to keep focused on student growth.
>
> *Assistant principal*

The second use of the principal portfolio is for summative evaluation. An external judgment of the effectiveness of the principal's leadership is made based on the artifacts and reflections included in the portfolio.

Career advancement is the third use of the principal portfolio. An innovative tool for pursuing leadership positions, seeking promotions, and assessing applicants, the artifacts and accompanying reflections represent strengths and accomplishments of the candidate that might not be apparent in the typical résumé, application form, or interview.

I developed a portfolio for career advancement purposes last year. This year I developed a portfolio for evaluative purposes. Though each is different in purpose, I can honestly say the reflection I did during the process made me grow professionally.

Elementary assistant principal

General Portfolio Benefits

The development of portfolios by students has been lauded by teachers and principals as especially useful in graphically portraying academic and creative abilities and in enhancing learning. Specific positive results of portfolio use among students include increased interest in learning, heightened motivation to achieve, and a stronger sense of self-responsibility for learning (Athanases, 1994; Buschman, 1993; Vizyak, 1994).

Teachers report that the use of portfolios enhances their own teaching, and they credit reflection for their considerable growth (Athanases, 1994; Tierney, 1993). Of additional importance to teacher growth is feedback and mentoring. Portfolios serve as a vehicle for providing feedback to teachers so that they may improve their teaching and level of professionalism (Doolittle, 1994). Brogan (1995) describes how portfolios may be used to provide teachers with the opportunity to grow professionally in concert with other teach-

---

When I began to pull my artifacts together and write reflections, I realized I had the skills to make a difference in teaching. I realized I *am* a good teacher.

Secondary teacher

---

ers and in ways that promote school, district, and student performance standards. Additional benefits for teachers include a sense of self-confidence, empowerment, and collegiality (Athanases, 1994; Bull, Montgomery, Coombs, Sebastian, & Fletcher, 1994). Furthermore, portfolios encourage collaboration; experimentation; incorporation of available knowledge bases; involvement in goal setting, evaluation, decision making, leadership and sustained administrative support, incentives, and rewards; and integration of individual goals with school and district goals (Brogan, 1995). Summarily, Brogan concludes that portfolios allow teachers to be in the middle of current efforts to improve the quality of teaching and learning in the schools.

In our analysis of the use of principal portfolios, we have observed similar results as those found among teachers. We have discovered that principals who engage in portfolio development enhance their professional growth, leadership skills, self-assessment skills, self-confidence, risk taking, professional dialogue and reading, goal setting, and integration of individual goals with campus and district goals. We have also observed that portfolios provide principals with a more individualized approach to evaluation and an effective tool for career advancement.

Needs and Benefits: For Professional Growth

As society has changed during the past few years, increased expectations of principals have emerged. Because principals represent the single most influential factor in promoting excellence in education (Lindahl, 1987), they have become more accountable, not only for their own performance but also for the performance of teachers, the achievement of students, and the involvement of parents and community. As expectations and accountability have increased, so has the principal's need to grow professionally.

Why is a professional growth portfolio needed? Professional growth enables principals to refine leadership practices and to increase school effectiveness. The professional growth portfolio serves as a catalyst for valuable self-reflection, providing direction for improvement in such areas as problem solving, collegial and community interactions, resource management, and, most important, student progress. Principals report that the analysis of past events assists them in becoming more proactive and developing valuable alternatives that enhance program effectiveness and improve schooling.

What are the benefits of a professional growth portfolio? According to principals, professional growth portfolios offer the following benefits:

- Assist in anticipating problems or conflicts
- Provide direction for improvement
- Provide for development of short-term and long-term goals
- Promote thoughtful actions or solutions to problems, rather than quick fixes or superficial solutions
- Assist in identification of needed resources
- Provide a nonthreatening structure for principal-to-principal coaching
- Promote data-based decision making
- Encourage risk taking and innovation
- Maintain the focus on student performance

My professional growth portfolio really helped me to think about using this process for evaluation purposes as well. As I reflected, for example, on a character program that we implemented this year, I found myself thinking about what would happen when the newness wears off or if teachers lose interest. What would be the benefit to the students? Then I thought about time for the teachers to reflect on and plan for the program. I really need to give them more time. I think my reflections here will bring about changes to the program—improvements. This is just one part of my professional growth portfolio that has helped me to grow. This demonstrates my leadership for the program and also could be part of my evaluation.

Junior high principal

Needs and Benefits: For Evaluation

Because of the myriad complexities of the principalship, the evaluation of principals is widely acknowledged to be challenging (Kroeze, 1984; Pellicer, Anderson, Keefe, Kelly, & McCleary, 1988; Shoemaker & Fraser, 1981; Sweeney, 1982). Current evaluation systems generally do not result in significant growth for the principal or the campus. The use of portfolios for evaluation of principals offers a new vision of evaluation.

Why is an evaluation portfolio needed? Principals perceive that, in general, evaluation systems do not promote professional growth or school improvement (Leithwood, 1987), do not relate to what con-

---

I didn't want to do the portfolio for evaluation unless we could really individualize it and base it on our goals for the year.

Elementary principal

---

tributes to principal effectiveness (Leithwood, 1987), lack a clear definition of job functions (DePree, 1974), are done *to* them rather than for or with them (DePree, 1974), prevent adaptive responses to problems (Lewis, 1982), are oriented to obsolete procedural checklists (DePree, 1974), are inconsistent and informal (Drake & Roe, 1994), and inhibit open communication and dialogue between evaluators and principals (Brown & Irby, 1996a). As a portfolio evaluation of principals is instituted, these negative perceptions of evaluation will be eliminated.

The thought of principal portfolios was a bit overwhelming in the beginning, but the principals selected this option for their evaluation. Now that we have moved through the storming, we can see great potential as we begin to internalize this process of using portfolios with our principals. The assistant superintendents will be serving as mentors, and there will be peer coaching among principals. This is seen as positive by the principals.

Assistant superintendent

What are the benefits of the evaluation portfolio for principals? The principal portfolio is a powerful evaluation tool that provides a positive, personal, and individualized approach to evaluation. Permitting both formative and summative evaluation, the portfolio provides comprehensive and authentic documentation typically not used in the principal's evaluation. This documentation presents a more realistic picture of principals' priorities and practices and offers valid insights into their leadership abilities. Assistant principals, principals, and superintendents report additional positive results from the use of portfolios in evaluation systems. They observe that portfolios

- Create ownership and commitment of the evaluation system at all administrative levels
- Address the need for improving schools at the campus level
- Promote open dialogue and collegiality from principal to principal as well as from principal to supervisor
- Allow principals to engage in and understand the development process prior to encouraging teachers to use portfolios for evaluation

- Focus on a "we-got-it" or "you-got-it" attitude, rather than a "gotcha" attitude
- Create a shared sense of leadership expectations
- Focus on strengths and allow the principal to relate those strengths during evaluation
- Encourage a more holistic view of evaluation

Needs and Benefits: For Career Advancement

Principals can use career advancement portfolios for advancing within the district or for seeking positions outside the district. The career advancement portfolio assists prospective employers in assessing principals' credentials, accomplishments, and potential.

Why is a career advancement portfolio needed? In the many career development seminars that we conduct, we find that individuals in a field of many qualified applicants are looking for a "competitive edge." The career advancement portfolio offers that competitive edge. Over and over, employers indicate that they hired the person who used a career advancement portfolio, or they indicate that that person made a great impression using the portfolio.

What are the benefits of the career advancement portfolio? When used for career advancement, portfolios provide principals with numerous positive benefits. Brown, Irby, Garrison, Shearer, and Smith (1996) report that the career advancement portfolio

- Offers visible evidence of leadership experiences and skills
- Enhances professional image
- Increases awareness of strengths and weaknesses
- Enhances self-confidence
- Assists in goal setting
- Promotes a thoughtful plan of remedial action and future development

All of the individuals I have interviewed who have used a portfolio seem confident. They know where they are going and how they can get there. They are also continuous learners.

High school principal

Summary

As we have worked with administrators on the development and use of portfolios, we have discovered that certain questions are asked more frequently than others. Resource A addresses those questions.

Portfolios address several specific needs of principals, particularly their need for reflection and professional growth, their need for an evaluation tool that is positive and relevant, and their need for a tool that can assist in career advancement. The ultimate challenge to the principal is improving student achievement and school effectiveness. Because portfolio development centers on change, it is a resource that can greatly enhance the principal's ability to meet this challenge.

As I see the power of reflection through the development of my portfolio, I have shared this with my teachers. I think the portfolio can change paradigms in schools.

Elementary principal

2

What Is Included in the Principal Portfolio?

Getting started on my portfolio was difficult. What would I put in it? Where would I start? When I began to think about what to place in the portfolio, it was overwhelming. Once I sat down and decided what I wanted to demonstrate, I became more focused and moved through the process. This was an excellent tool for me to think about my practice and accomplishments.

Elementary principal

Although portfolios are generally well known among students and teachers, only recently have principals begun to use portfolios to document their experiences, expertise, and progress in leadership. Because principal portfolios can be used for several purposes—professional growth and self-assessment, evaluation, or career advancement—artifacts and accompanying reflections, as well as style, will vary depending on the portfolio's intended use.

This chapter answers several general questions regarding the appearance and contents of the principal portfolio. Each principal will determine specific contents and style to personalize his or her portfolio and to accomplish its intended purpose.

What Should the Portfolio Look Like?

Determining the physical, organizational, and conceptual structure of the portfolio, whatever its intended use, is the first step. We have worked with some administrators on the development of electronic portfolios. Of course, the appearance of an electronic portfolio would be different from the paper portfolios we describe in this section. Because the portfolio represents the principal to the reader, it is important to portray a professional image and to invite review. The portfolio should be arranged in a logical and readable manner with its organization readily apparent and should always include a table of contents that lists each section with page numbers. Sections should be clearly indicated; tabbed pages or color-coded dividers are commonly used. Generally, the portfolio is arranged in a zippered three-ring binder; this adds to the attractiveness and professional appearance of the portfolio and makes it easier for both the reviewer and the creator to handle. When typing portfolio entries or section page dividers, attention should be given to the font size and style. It is recommended that an easy-to-read, professional font be selected and that it not be changed unless the altered form is used for emphasis or adds to the attractiveness of the portfolio.

I advise that a nice black binder can be used for the portfolio, just as well as an expensive leather zippered one. I went to the local supercenter and purchased my notebook and spent less than $5.

Administrative assistant

How Should the Portfolio Development Process Begin?

Principals who have not developed the habit of keeping samples of their work will need to begin to do so. Many administrators find that the most efficient method for collecting potential artifacts is to create file folders related to various areas or criteria of leadership or various aspects of their role and then simply place all samples into the designated file.

Once a collection of artifacts is in place, selection of artifacts for inclusion is crucial. It will be necessary to prioritize. Although the portfolio must be comprehensive enough to portray a wide range of experiences and competencies and to present a true picture of the individual's values and leadership styles, the creator may not have the luxury of including several artifacts to represent one skill or leadership area. This will necessitate choosing which one or two entries constitute the most effective representation.

> A colleague of mine and I created a file folder for each of the criteria in our evaluation system. We had a hanging folder in our desk drawer for problem solving, curriculum and instruction, staff development, budgeting, collaboration, etc. Every time we had anything related to one we just dropped it in the folder. In June, when it was time to analyze our performance for the entire year, we simply went through the artifacts, selected two from each area that really represented what we thought demonstrated that we had met the district criteria, and developed our reflections.
>
> *Elementary principal*

How Lengthy Should the Portfolio Be?

It is important to remember that the portfolio should be comprehensive enough to represent the creator while succinctly and effectively conveying the intended message. Although the portfolio should be broad in scope—documenting relevant experiences, leadership areas, or goals—this is a case where "less may be more." A portfolio that is too lengthy or bulky could create a negative psychological impression, failing to invite the reviewer to carefully read it as well as portraying a lack of consideration of the reviewer's time.

> After I had developed an outline of the sections I wanted to include in my portfolio, I went through boxes of artifacts to find the very best example.
>
> *Preservice secondary principal*

What Are the Component Parts?

Even though the specific contents and styles of portfolios may vary depending on purpose and individual preference, certain components are almost always included.

Table of Contents

The first item in the portfolio, the table of contents, should indicate clearly how the portfolio is organized. A table of contents is illustrated in Figure 2.1.

<table>
<tr><td colspan="2" align="center">**Table of Contents**</td></tr>
<tr><td>Introduction</td><td>1</td></tr>
<tr><td>Résumé</td><td>2</td></tr>
<tr><td>Leadership Framework</td><td>4</td></tr>
<tr><td>Five-Year Goals</td><td>7</td></tr>
<tr><td>Section 1: Learner-Centered Leadership</td><td>8</td></tr>
<tr><td>Section 2: Curriculum & Instruction</td><td>10</td></tr>
<tr><td>Section 3: Effective Communication</td><td>13</td></tr>
<tr><td>Section 4: Building a Learning Community</td><td>15</td></tr>
<tr><td>Section 5: Fiscal Accountability</td><td>20</td></tr>
<tr><td>Accolades</td><td>23</td></tr>
<tr><td>Vita</td><td>28</td></tr>
</table>

Figure 2.1. Sample Table of Contents for the Career Advancement Portfolio

Introduction or Overview

The first section, probably no more than one page, explains the purpose and organization of the portfolio and also briefly introduces the principal to the reader. For example, the introduction of a career advancement portfolio might look like this:

This portfolio outlines my accomplishments in leadership during the past 3 years of my tenure as principal of Oakland Elementary School. Not only will the reader find my current résumé, but also my Leadership Framework, 5-year goals, and vita. Furthermore, I have divided the remaining sections into the leadership areas of problem analysis, community relations, and staff development, the three major components of the director of staff development position for which I am applying.

Résumé

A current résumé should be included next. Some individuals choose to place a résumé at the beginning of the portfolio and a vita, which presents at length details of their professional career, at the end of the portfolio. The résumé illustrated in Figure 2.2 is a model that we have advocated in our leadership seminars and includes an objective (if the résumé is used in the career advancement portfolio) and a listing of certifications or endorsements, education, experience, areas of concentration, and strengths.

Leadership Framework

The Leadership Framework[1] is a summarization of the primary beliefs and attitudes of the administrator regarding leadership. If the principal has not developed such a framework, it is necessary to do so prior to continuing with the development of the portfolio.

The creation of the framework is the first written reflective action in portfolio development. All other reflections are predicated on the beliefs about leadership expressed in the framework. Articulating the Leadership Framework is important for several reasons. First, the writing of the framework compels the principal to reflect on his or her philosophy of leadership, learning, and teaching. Second, the framework provides a structure for reflection on what the principal does and why he or she does it, ultimately allowing the principal to assess his or her beliefs as they relate to district and campus expectations, practices, and norms. Finally, a clearly articulated Leadership Framework conveys to faculty, colleagues, and others who the principal is and what the principal "stands for" and expects.

> Developing my Leadership Framework was difficult because I had to really think about my core values. That took some time, but I'm glad I did it. When I went to the job interview, I didn't have to think about what I believed, like my philosophy—I could quickly tell the interviewer.
>
> *Elementary curriculum coordinator*

John Garza
232 Bluebird Lane
Houston, TX 77555
713-555-5555

Objective:

> To serve Jones Public Schools by responsibly and professionally directing all operations as Elementary Principal at Jones Elementary School.

Professional Qualifications/Education/Additional Training*

M.Ed.	University of Utah, Salt Lake City, Utah, 1990
M.S.	University del Valle, Guatemala, C.A., 1974
B.S.	Universidad de San Carlos, Guatemala, C.A., 1972
*July, 1995	Portfolio Development, Sam Houston State University, Huntsville, Texas
*July, 1994	Change Facilitation, SEDL, Austin, Texas
*June, 1993	The Seven Habits of Highly Effective People, Covey Facilitator Training, Provo, Utah
*June, 1989	Grantwriting Workshop, University of Utah, Salt Lake City, Utah

Chronological Employment History

August, 1991–Present	Assistant Principal, Happy Day Elementary, Jones Public Schools, Houston, Texas
August, 1988–August, 1991	Director of the Bilingual/ESL Programs, Logan Public Schools, Salt Lake City, Utah
August, 1984–August, 1988	Teacher, Bilingual Education, Logan Public Schools, Salt Lake City, Utah
August, 1974–August, 1984	Supervisor, The American School, Guatemala, C.A.
August, 1972–August, 1974	Teacher and Director, Paramos Rural School, Paramos, Guatemala, C.A.

Areas of Concentration

> Leadership Development, Public Relations, Cultural Diversity, Family Literacy, Bilingual Education, Mathematics Development, Science Inquiry Approaches

Strengths

> Student-Centered, Bilingual in English and Spanish, Team Builder, Program Evaluation, Change Facilitation, Grant Writing and Acquisition (funded grants total > $2,000,000)

Figure 2.2. Sample Résumé

Following are seven suggested components of the Leadership Framework and an explanation of each:

1. *Philosophy of education.* This component provides insights into basic beliefs about the purposes of education and the importance of schools to society. This forms the foundation not only for the principal's practice but also for subsequent components of the framework.

> Like most educators, I had written many philosophies of education. The Leadership Framework gave me a structure to examine and share my beliefs in a much more comprehensive and meaningful way.
>
> *Elementary curriculum coordinator*

2. *Philosophy of leadership.* What the principal believes about effective leadership and its impact is stated here. Questions such as, What constitutes effective, purposeful leadership? and How is effective, purposeful leadership sustained? are addressed.

3. *Vision for learners.* An in-depth analysis of what the principal believes about how children or adolescents learn and about his or her role in promoting learning is essential to the development of this component.

4. *Vision for teachers.* Here the principal examines and shares his or her views on teachers: what it means to be a teacher, what a teacher's role is in lives of children in the classroom and within the campus community, and how teachers should relate to students and others.

5. *Vision for the organization.* A discussion of the principal's vision for the organization or school campus is important because this provides an image of how the principal thinks the campus "should be or could be." Within this component, the principal should comment on

- Climate
- Community
- Collaboration
- Communication

> The development of my Leadership Framework was a difficult task. I'm glad I did it; it made me really dig deep into my soul and think about how I really felt about education, schools, and leadership. I review it often to make sure that I am practicing what I say I believe.
>
> *Intermediate assistant principal*

6. *Vision for professional growth.* How the principal feels about professional growth affects student achievement and the effectiveness of

schools. Here the principal discusses views on the significance of professional development for himself or herself and for the faculty as well as how professional growth needs will be determined and addressed.

7. *Method of vision attainment.* All visions are merely cryptic illusions unless there is a strategy for obtaining the vision. In discussing how they will move the organization toward the vision, principals will need to address the following:

- Decision making
- Encouragement, initiation, and facilitation of change
- Support during change

Although the Leadership Framework should be comprehensive, it should not be lengthy. One or two paragraphs for each component is sufficient. Figure 2.3 on pages 17 and 18 offers an example of an elementary principal's Leadership Framework.

Five-Year Goals

The inclusion of personal leadership goals in the portfolio conveys to readers that the principal knows where he or she needs to go and has a plan for getting there. This section is simply a one-page listing of the principal's goals for the next 5 years. Helpful questions include: What are my personal administrative plans for the next 5 years? Where do I see myself in the future? What contributions do I see myself making? What is important to me in my profession and how can I accomplish this through a 5-year plan? Figure 2.4 presents the goals of a middle school principal.

Within the next 5 years, I plan to accomplish the following goals:

1. Create a school climate where there are high expectations for students and teachers
2. Be proactive rather than reactive in responding to situations and issues
3. Secure funds for integrating the arts into the curriculum
4. Secure funds for intensive staff development sessions based on the needs of the campus
5. Form study teams on the campus

Figure 2.4. Sample of 5-Year Goals

Leadership Framework
John Garza
Department Chair
Jones School District

Philosophy of Education
There are three basic reasons for education. First, to prepare children for life in a democratic society by providing them with key concepts from all academic disciplines. Second, to instill an understanding of the values of our society, the difference between right and wrong, the idea that life choices have consequences, and the self-discipline and self-esteem that accompany that understanding. Third, to equip students with the tools to become lifelong learners.

Philosophy of Leadership
The principal is the instructional leader of the building. Of all the models of supervision available, the human resources model is the most effective. In this approach, the principal will view satisfaction as a desirable end toward which teachers will work. Also, sharing of the decision-making process between administrators and teachers is vital in order to increase school effectiveness.

Vision for Learners
Every child deserves a chance to learn, and every child is a learner. It is apparent that not every child can or will learn in the same way. Therefore, it is important to teach to the individual child and the whole child. Material must be presented in a variety of ways for optimum learning. In order for all to learn, children need to know that they are valued and that they have strengths to build on and weaknesses to overcome. It is the responsibility of the principal and teacher to provide each child with a supportive, student-centered learning environment.

Vision for Teachers
Teachers are at the heart of the child's learning system. They are supporters, encouragers, and facilitators of learning. Teachers must have time to plan together and alone so that effective programs are developed for students. Teachers are accountable for motivating each child in the classroom. Teachers should be provided with supportive words and resources, including materials, assistants, time, and money to do their jobs effectively. They should be in an ongoing program of staff development.

Vision for the Organization
The organization should be a place that prepares children to be lifelong learners. It should be a system where teachers feel like they have an active role in the decision-making process, where parents are involved in their child's education, and where school is seen as a vital part of the community. The organization is in a constant state of evolution as the needs of students change. The vision and commitment of the administrator leads to a domino effect that affects the faculty, the students, and the community. The result is an organization where high expectations lead to higher achievement for all.

(continued)

Figure 2.3. Sample Leadership Framework

Vision for Professional Growth

I believe that professional growth and staff development is the ongoing and job-related program within the school district that is designed to maintain and define the required competencies of the district's employees. Supervisors should not merely transmit expectations for teacher performance and then evaluate the extent to which teachers conform to those expectations, however. Since the main thrust of adult education should be self-determination, the principal must provide a supportive, nonthreatening environment where teachers, together with the principal, can develop a plan for improvement. This plan will be the result of honest self-diagnosis on the part of the teacher and a measuring of the gaps that exist between present teaching competencies and ideal states. This can be related to a principal's growth as well.

Method of Vision Attainment

A principal cannot undertake the task of creating a first-rate educational community by him or herself. He or she must enlist the help of the community by cultivating productive relationships with parents and business leaders. Also, staffing skills will be needed in order to attract and keep innovative teachers and dismiss those who fail to meet high expectations of the organization. It is important to balance the traits of both classical and human relations theorists, to be both task-oriented and receptive to the needs of the faculty. Ultimately, the principal must perform seven special functions—planning, staffing, organizing, directing, coordinating, reporting, and budgeting—with the success of the students in mind. It is only then that the ultimate vision of the organization—the best possible education for all students—will be realized.

Figure 2.3. Sample Leadership Framework, Continued

Artifacts and Reflections

Once I started finding artifacts that went along with the criteria and my goals and started writing and working through the analysis of my work for the year, I really saw the things I had spent my time on! This was significant for me because I found out that I needed to be spending more time on my communication skills.

Middle school principal

This component is the heart of the portfolio, because it is this component that provides authentic examples of the principal's work and the principal's interpretation of the effect or significance of his or her work. This documentation and interpretation provides critical information to the reviewer regarding the abilities, professionalism, and character of the principal. The remainder of the portfolio consists of the artifacts and reflections representing areas of leadership the principal or central administrators wish to emphasize. A list of artifacts and an accompanying reflection are found in Figure 2.5.

Artifacts and reflections are placed in sections generally organized around leadership skills or proficiencies, district or campus

Criteria:	Staff development
Goals:	To develop a catalog of potential staff development topics for advanced teachers
	To develop a long-term staff development calendar with beginning teachers, along with their mentors
	To develop staff development plans for all staff members, including secretarial and support service staff
	To develop a personal staff development plan
Artifacts:	Page of catalog
	Calendar for beginning teachers
	Sample staff development plan
	Personal development plan

I selected these artifacts because they are representative of all the work that has been put in by the staff and myself on the accomplishment of these goals. First of all, during our faculty (all), parent (10), student (10), support staff (5) 2-day retreat, I introduced my goals for staff development for the year. Afterward, we divided into teams to develop strategies for accomplishing the goals. I allowed the teams to prioritize the budget and restructure it as needed to accomplish this end. (I met with the business manager to review a restructured budget.) We also used the Joyce and Showers book, *Student Achievement Through Staff Development*, as we began and worked through our tasks. Some of the groups felt they needed more information, so they convened at the campus to secure that information. Additionally, each group was charged with developing a plan to assess the impact of the staff development for the year. I worked on my personal growth plan and got feedback from each group (see plan). The staff development goals were met by each group.

According to the evaluation systems designed by the groups, the advanced teachers (senior teachers/master teachers on my campus) attended an average of two conferences/workshops during the year. They, in turn, as indicated by the plan, had to conduct action research in their classroom with the information and report to the faculty. The accomplishments were reported in May during the faculty retreat. Reports are available as parents walk into the office or for teachers to check out. The group decided this was a good model for beginning or midlevel teachers. The mentor teachers and beginning teachers worked together through a combined effort in staff development. They formed inquiry groups and sharing groups, and also went to staff development meetings together in the region. The new mentors attended a workshop prepared by former mentors on how to mentor. A pre-post assessment was given to beginning teachers and to mentors regarding attitudes. Attitudes toward mentoring were 98% favorable. Other items of note are filed in my office. The group also compared the first-year scores of students in previous years of beginning teachers who did not have mentors who were consistently mentoring appropriately, and the scores for this group were 30% higher.

The secretarial staff and custodial staff, as well as the support service staff, have never before been involved in staff development. Their reports are extremely favorable and need to have additional study. They attended one staff development during the year (20 staff members) and were able to meet together as sharing groups on a formal basis (time was provided).

(continued)

Figure 2.5. Sample of an Artifact and Reflection

During the year I attended three staff development sessions conducted by ASCD in curriculum alignment issues and NASSP/NAESP leadership. Overall, this year our scores improved by 5 percentage points on the state evaluation, which placed us in a recognized category. I plan to implement a peer coaching system next year as one of my goals. That was discussed in all inquiry groups this year with a staff developer coming in an discussing those issues with us, as well as our reading about the subject. We all believe that this can help us to become an exemplary school.

Figure 2.5. Sample of an Artifact and Reflection, Continued

goals, or the principal's personal goals for the campus. For example, in an evaluation portfolio, the district may require that three particular leadership proficiencies, such as general leadership, staff development, and curriculum and instruction, be addressed. Under each of these proficiencies are indicators that serve as guides for goal setting. Each of the three proficiencies will be supported by artifacts and accompanying reflections that are linked to the goals that have been set by the principal. Figure 2.6 depicts such a schema; Figure 2.7 provides a list of potential artifacts.

The structure Drs. Brown and Irby gave us to complete our portfolio made it easier to think about it and to put it together. One thing I know I would do differently is to keep as many samples of things I do as possible. So many of the people in the seminar, like me, had not thought that was important. And it wasn't, until now. I see the worth in this type of portfolio.

Assistant principal

Portfolio development requires much thought, time, and effort. The guidelines in this chapter should make the initial task less overwhelming and cumbersome. Once the principal has developed a schema for developing a portfolio, updating and altering the portfolio for various purposes is not nearly as laborious or time-consuming.

Note

1. The Leadership Framework is based on the work of Schon (1993), Sergiovanni and Starratt (1988), and Walker (1971).

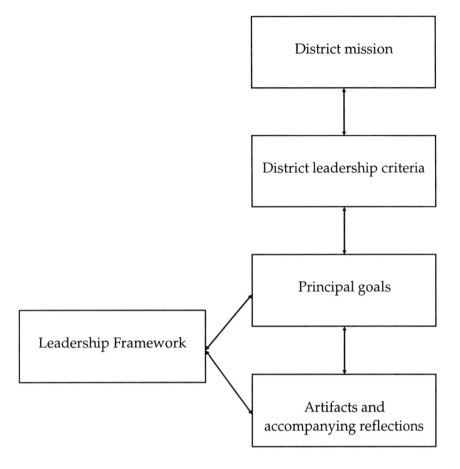

Figure 2.6. Connected Schema of the Reflections to District Criteria

Agendas of meetings conducted
Outlines and evaluations of staff development sessions
Letters of appreciation
Pages from a curriculum document
Notes on peer coaching
Schedules or certificates of attendance at professional meetings, conferences, or staff
    development sessions
A proposed budget for a project
A long-range plan or action plan for implementing a program change or curriculum revision
Research or evaluation report
Letters of commendation or support from parents, colleagues, and supervisors

Figure 2.7. Suggested Artifacts to Include in the Career Advancement Portfolio

3

The Principal Portfolio for Professional Growth

> Before I worked through the portfolio, I didn't do much thinking about what really constituted my leadership behavior. I didn't really listen inwardly to myself and look at my impact on teachers and students on my campus. The portfolio forced me to reflect and, I believe, move to a higher level of leadership.
>
> *Junior high principal*

Much of the current literature on successful leadership emphasizes the importance of reflection to improving the organization. The greatest benefit derived from administrative portfolio development is realized through the process of reflection, as the principal assesses the effectiveness and impact of his or her leadership beliefs, style, and practices. The reflection inherent in the portfolio development process: (a) provides insights into strengths and weaknesses, (b) encourages planning for professional growth, (c) leads to improved practice by the principal, and (d) ultimately enhances school and teacher effectiveness and improves student learning. This chapter focuses on the principal's professional growth. It describes the reflective principal and suggests a structure for developing written reflections.

Reflection for Professional Improvement

The principal's job is multifaceted, demanding, fast-paced, and in some instances, stressful and chaotic. Although it is difficult to find the time to step back and analyze decisions and subsequent actions, it is critical that the principal do so. Research on effective principals (Leithwood & Stager, 1986) indicates that highly effective principals are reflective, particularly regarding problem solving and their overall leadership style. Because it compels principals to examine critically their own leadership beliefs, behaviors, and experiences, the portfolio is a catalyst for this much needed and valuable reflection.

Research on student and teacher portfolios has proven conclusively that self-assessment is essential for growth. In fact, in their investigations of teacher reflection, Grant and Zeichner (1984) learned that teachers who do not reflect "lose sight of the fact that their everyday reality is only one of many possible alternatives. They tend to forget the purposes and ends toward which they are working" (p. 4). If this is true for teachers, then principals, too, are in some danger of losing focus and of overlooking possible alternatives. Principals who have been involved with the development of portfolios report that the processes of selecting viable samples of work and writing accompanying reflections have been beneficial in denoting areas of needed improvement, in assisting in maintaining focus, and in providing new perspectives and creative insights.

> I need to alter my leadership approaches in order to advance my goals. I can see now how some of my actions have not truly advanced the goals that I set for this school year.
>
> *Intermediate school principal*

The Reflective Principal

As we have assisted administrators in the development and use of portfolios, we have discovered the following commonalities among reflective administrators:

1. *View self-assessment and reflection as priorities for school improvement.* Reflective principals recognize the importance of reflection to improving their schools. They believe that to improve their own performance, and ultimately, student performance, they must make self-assessment an integral part of their routine. These principals draw on their intuitive understandings about their practice, seek out new understandings regarding the particular problem at hand, and connect those intuitive thoughts with new ones. The results of this kind of reflective practice are improved schools. In addition, reflective principals model the reflective process and are commonly observed coaching their teachers in the process.

2. *Recognize that external and internal challenges result in growth.* As administrators self-assess, they investigate and interpret their actions or practices. Refusing to rely merely on traditional solutions or approaches, they actively explore alternatives and typically create new answers or ways to approach problems. Additionally, reflective practitioners solicit feedback from others that questions, challenges, or seeks to clarify their actions or decisions. Because they realize that feedback and dialogue can validate personal constructions and result in growth, they constantly seek input on their most critical challenge: What impact has my leadership made on the lives of teachers and students, as well as on the school and the community at large?

> I have found one of the most positive things about being trained in the portfolio development process is the dialogue with fellow principals in the district. We have learned so much from each other about how to improve our practice on our individual campuses. We never thought about how powerful dialogue could be.
>
> *Junior high principal*

3. *Intentionally engage in activities aimed at challenging current beliefs and practice and expanding understandings.* Reflective principals recognize

that to improve the process of schooling, they must enrich and deepen their own understanding regarding current theory and best practice through reading widely, attending relevant professional meetings and workshops, joining study or focus groups, and seeking discussion with colleagues.

4. *Understand that change is inevitable.* Reflective principals accept that they, their staff, and their campus must change as circumstances, events, and the environment change and as new information becomes available. As they facilitate change for growth, relevancy, and currency, they keep in mind the challenges to an individual or organization moving through the change process. They facilitate change by experimenting with various alternatives; they support change by making available needed resources and by remaining flexible and adaptable.

5. *Recognize that chaos often accompanies change.* Reflective principals understand that changes on a campus or within a district may create disruptions or dissonance and that the potential for chaos exists. Anticipating this aspect of change, they advance current knowledge toward new solutions, provide a stabilizing influence for their faculties and staff, and do not allow the organization to be deterred from its mission.

6. *Share understandings with colleagues.* Reflective principals are eager to share new learnings and ideas with teachers, staff, and colleagues. They make time to dialogue with other principals, and they tend to coach and mentor new administrators.

The six attributes described above serve as benchmarks for principals who are interested in engaging in reflection to inform their practice. Figure 3.1, the Reflective Performance Scale, assists readers in identifying to what degree they possess these attributes.

Structure for Developing Reflective Practice

Because some administrators with whom we have worked have limited experience in the development of their own portfolios, they have indicated that in the initial stages a structure for approaching the

Carefully review the activities below. Place a check in the box that best describes the frequency with which you perform the activity.

Activity	Seldom	Sometimes	Often
Plans time for reflection	☐	☐	☐
Plans to improve personal performance	☐	☐	☐
Maintains professional growth orientation	☐	☐	☐
Critiques own behaviors and interactions	☐	☐	☐
Solicits feedback on behavior and performance	☐	☐	☐
Explores alternatives to challenges	☐	☐	☐
Determines where improvements can be made	☐	☐	☐
Analyzes impact of behaviors/decisions on others	☐	☐	☐
Seeks and uses data to forecast needed changes	☐	☐	☐
Adapts to change when needed	☐	☐	☐
Continues change efforts to achieve success	☐	☐	☐
Encourages teachers and staff to reflect	☐	☐	☐
Encourages continuation of positive performance	☐	☐	☐
Shares understandings with faculty and colleagues	☐	☐	☐
Maintains focus on goals	☐	☐	☐
Modifies actions/beliefs based on reflections	☐	☐	☐

Total your check marks in each column: ____   ____   ____

(*Seldom* total ___ × 1 = ___) + (*Sometimes* total ___ × 2 = ___) + (*Often* total ___ × 3 = ___) = _____
                                                                                        Total score

Rating for reflective performance
   Up to 41 points = Need for improvement is indicated
   42 to 44 points = Average to above average performance is indicated
   45 to 48 points = Qualities of a reflective administrator are indicated

Figure 3.1. Reflective Performance Scale
SOURCE: Brown, Irby, and Chance (1996). Used with permission.

reflection process is helpful. Principals report that the use of the reflection cycle (Brown & Irby, 1996b), depicted in Figure 3.2, has enhanced their ability and their confidence in developing written reflections to accompany artifacts included in their portfolios (Brown & Irby, 1996a).

Reflections are highly individualized. They vary according to the purpose of the portfolio and the areas of emphasis, the principal's judgment, preferences, experiences, thought processes, and writing

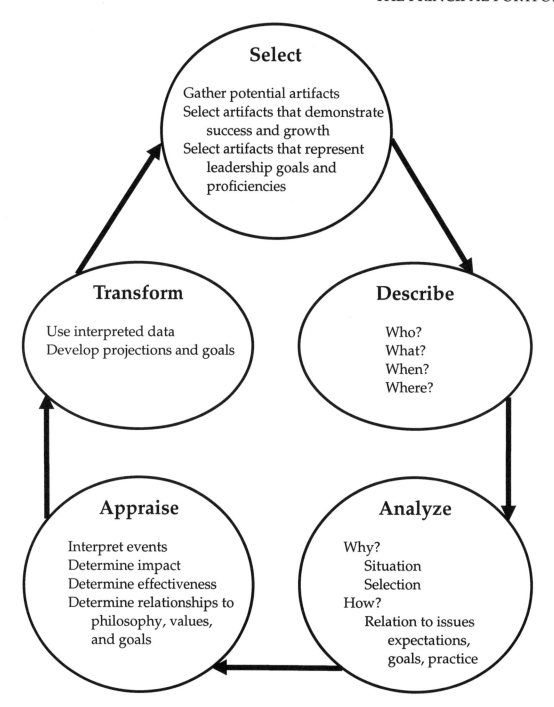

Figure 3.2. The Administrative Reflection Cycle (the Reflection Cycle)
SOURCE: Brown and Irby (1996b). Used with permission.

style. The reflection cycle offers a structure that, although somewhat prescriptive, allows for individuality. The steps are intended to serve as a general outline, and the suggested questions serve as prompts to assist in the actual writing of the reflections that will accompany the artifacts in the portfolio. As principals move through the stages of reflection, they will not necessarily answer every question.

Step 1—Select. The principal must first select the artifacts most representative of the leadership goals or proficiencies that he or she is attempting to demonstrate. For example, in an evaluation portfolio, if one of the principal's goals relates to some aspect of staff development, then the principal will select an artifact(s) most clearly illustrative of success or growth in this area. In this step the principal will ask

> The structure allows me to put my reflections into a written format easily so that my superintendent can see the impact I have had on my campus. He cannot be there throughout this process and does not see the progress that has really been made.
>
> *Elementary principal*

What documents or artifacts most graphically represent my involvement or activities in a particular area?

Which artifacts relate directly to the goal or proficiency and demonstrate success and/or growth?

Which artifacts reveal the most about my capabilities or skills in this area?

Step 2—Describe. A description of the circumstances, situation, or events related to the experience is included in this step. Four "W" questions are usually addressed:

Who was involved?

What were the circumstances, concerns, or issues?

When did the event or series of events occur?

Where did this take place?

Step 3—Analyze. This step involves "digging deeper." The "why" of the selection of the artifact and the "how" of its relationship to the events, leadership issues or beliefs, circumstances, and/or decisions occur. Appropriate questions include

Why is this artifact representative of the goal, accomplishment, or issue?

Why is the situation represented in this artifact significant in demonstrating competency?

How does this artifact relate to personal, district, or campus
goals? To leadership expectations, skills, or beliefs?

How is the vision developed and shared?

How is collaboration facilitated?

How is feedback provided and received?

How are resources managed and organized?

How are plans developed and implemented?

How are decisions made and acted on?

Step 4—Appraise. In the previous three steps, the principal has described and analyzed the experience. The actual self-assessment
occurs in Step 4 as the principal interprets the events, evaluates the
impact and appropriateness of his or her action(s), and relates them
to his or her values and beliefs. Suggested guiding questions are

Did the action(s) taken result in the intended outcomes?

Were the actions effective and appropriate for the situation?

Were the actions consistent with the espoused Leadership
Framework?

What impact did decisions or actions have on students, teachers, and/or the community?

Is this leadership behavior representative of district expectations?

Were options derived from multiple perspectives considered?

Were a variety of alternatives considered?

Was the very best course of action taken?

How might this situation have been approached in a different
manner? And what types of results might be expected?

What action(s) might have resulted in a more positive impact?

How does this experience promote growth?

Step 5—Transform. This step holds the greatest opportunity for growth as
the principal uses insights gained from reflection in developing plans
designed to improve and transform practice. Here the principal asks

What actions and decisions will move the organization be-
yond standard expectations?

What activities will enhance skills, methodologies, and strategies?

What activities will deepen understandings of relevant issues, practices, theories, and research studies?

How does this experience help to improve practice?

What plan for improvement of student learning can be developed from the interpreted data?

Has reflection resulted in a need to alter the Leadership Framework?

Principal Reflections

The principal reflection in Figure 3.3 illustrates the use of the five steps in the reflection cycle.

Reflection by the principal necessitates the engagement in thoughtful and careful reporting and analysis of past practices, events, and experiences, thus offering valuable insights into one's leadership progress. Reflection takes the principal from a basic level of acceptance of the way things are in the process of schooling to a level of critical examination, self-assessment, and new visions. The portfolio provides impetus for principals to reflect actively on their leading and learning and to make plans for enhanced principal, teacher, and school effectiveness, which leads to improved student achievement.

Portfolio development requires time and commitment. It not only requires time to select artifacts, it also requires time to write reflections and to develop alternative plans. Although the amount of time required could be considered a negative aspect of portfolio development, our work with principals has indicated that when they believe portfolio development will make a difference in their performance and in their schools and when they have ownership in the development of the portfolios, supportive environments in which to use them, and the necessary resources, principals commit to the process and invest the energy and time required.

> I thought about reflection. I can reflect on my experiences, but without action coming from the reflection, the reflection is nothing more than a daydream.
>
> *Elementary principal*

Criteria: Leadership

Goal: To develop a shared vision or mission for the campus

Artifacts: An agenda from a meeting with staff
                   An agenda from a meeting with parents
                   An agenda from a meeting with students
                   The mission of the school   [Select]

These artifacts represent my working toward a shared vision or mission for the campus. I selected 20 individuals from each of the above-mentioned groups, randomly, to meet in six separate meetings but opened up the meetings to anyone who would also be interested. During the meetings, I sought their input for the development of the school's mission. We met during the months of September and October. Since my school serves three small and widespread communities, I met with the parents during night meetings in these communities at three churches. The staff and student meetings were held on the campus.   [Describe]

These artifacts are important documents that demonstrate my ability to lead a group toward the development of a shared mission and vision for the school. As the reader can see, the first three artifacts led up to the fourth artifact, which is the developed mission. Each campus was required by the district to have a mission for the campus. The district did not require that the mission be shared; however, my philosophy is one of collaboration. Therefore, it was important for me to involve all stakeholders in the students' education. I held the parent meetings in the communities, since they are far from the school and it is difficult for parents to come to the campus at night. Through this process, other areas of need for the campus were identified.   [Analyze]

My experience during this process led me to see that collaboration is important. Because there were 100 parents involved in the development of the mission for the school, we are having much better parent support. The developed mission has directed us in a path of change, and we have already begun to develop an action plan for those changes. One of the changes is a newly developed campus team that includes four parents, four teachers, and two students, who are now working on a campus action plan. This continued collaboration, as well as a feedback loop (developed by the campus team to get continued input), is crucial to solving problems. I feel that the process we used to develop the action plan was effective and that the plan itself will meet our needs. Items addressed in the action plan are student motivation, parent involvement, staff development on improving test scores, and gang involvement prevention. Additionally, the action plan includes more involvement activities for the community and parents and teachers to develop subplans for improvement on the campus.   [Appraise]

I am supportive of the changes that have been brought about through this collaborative process. I am trying to facilitate these changes through the reallocation of some budget items. In fact, I have redirected some of the budget in staff development to substitutes for teachers who need to be freed for planning days. We will continue to plan this year, with all action plans placed into effect during the next school term.   [Transform]

Figure 3.3. Sample Principal Reflection Indicating Components of the Reflection Cycle

4

The Principal Portfolio for Evaluation

I used the portfolio to evaluate my assistant principals this year. They were able to keep focused on their goals and were able to articulate how they attained their goals in the portfolio. This type of evaluation gave me an excellent view of the leadership that my assistant principals exhibited this year.

Intermediate principal

Evaluation of principals is challenging. Despite the fact that principal evaluation instruments and systems have received attention during the past few years and have been considerably polished and improved, widespread dissatisfaction still exists. Administrators agree that a new vision of principal evaluation is needed. This chapter describes the evaluation portfolio, offers advantages of the use of the evaluation portfolio, suggests contents of the evaluation portfolio, and discusses how the evaluation portfolio might be presented.

The Evaluation Portfolio

When we started using the evaluation portfolio in our district, it was hard to conceive of how this could help us, but as we delved into it and looked at how it was so different from our old checklist, we began to see how this could authenticate our evaluations.

Elementary principal

Although the evaluation portfolio has much in common with the other two types of portfolios, it is created specifically for external review. The aim of principals in designing the evaluation portfolio is to present concrete evidence that their leadership performance meets or exceeds district expectations and results in positive outcomes for students, teachers, and the community. Artifacts and accompanying reflections in the evaluation portfolio relate specifically to criteria or goals specified by the district's evaluation system.

Advantages of the Evaluation Portfolio

The tasks of the principal have expanded as the principalship has evolved. The principal has not been relieved of a single role but has accumulated additional roles and responsibilities as the field of education has expanded. Today the principalship has taken on dimensions that defy the grasp and capabilities of a single individual (Harrison & Peterson, 1986).

Not only does the multifaceted nature of principals' work make evaluation problematic, even when more specific functions are mandated, much ambiguity remains. For example, the school effectiveness literature emphasizes a number of functions for principals that are extremely difficult to operationalize. Constructs that have emerged such as school climate, high expectations, coordination and organization, and instructional leadership do not easily lend themselves to traditional evaluation practices (Kroeze, 1984; Shoemaker & Fraser, 1981; Sweeney, 1982). The fact that current leadership theory emphasizes that leading any organization is both contingent and situational (Hoy & Miskel, 1987) further challenges existing evaluation systems. New definitions of leadership effectiveness include moral dimensions of leadership with emphasis on the promotion of higher values and purposes. Existing evaluation systems cannot adequately evaluate principals on the leadership functions or constructs listed above.

What is an effective evaluation system? Several basic assumptions concerned with principal evaluation are advanced by Redfern (1972, 1980):

> I look forward to getting to share what I have been doing. Really, before now the central administration had no idea all the things I did for my campus.
>
> *Junior high principal*

- The principal's productivity can and should be evaluated.
- The principal should understand what is expected.
- The principal should know to whom he or she should go for direction and supervision.
- Standards of excellence should be designed against which to measure performance.
- Performance objectives should be formulated cooperatively between the principal and his or her evaluator.
- The principal should be evaluated on general leadership functions and on the specific work he or she has been assigned.

The use of the evaluation portfolio, as a basic element in a larger evaluation system, overcomes many of the deficiencies of current evaluation systems and meets the requirements of effective evaluation systems listed above. The evaluation portfolio provides for principals and supervisors to collaboratively develop and agree on standards, expectations, goals, and/or proficiencies to be evaluated and directly addresses those standards, expectations, goals, and/or proficiencies. Principals are able to work with their supervisors during the formative evaluation stage as the supervisors offer clarification and assistance. The artifacts and reflections included in the evaluation portfolio allow the principal to demonstrate strengths, not only in general leadership functions but on specific work as well. Because principals select the evidence that most accurately represents what they do, they are able to address the fragmented, ambiguous, and situational nature of their specific work. Congruence of the principal's practices with his or her values or beliefs is encouraged through the development and use of the evaluation portfolio as principals analyze their behaviors and activities in relationship to statements included in their Leadership Framework. Figure 4.1 contrasts traditional evaluation systems with the evaluation portfolio.

Contents of the Evaluation Portfolio

Components of the evaluation portfolio may vary based on district requirements; however, most of the components of the principal portfolio discussed in Chapter 2 are generally included in evaluation portfolios. The résumé and Leadership Framework are usually the first two items developed for the evaluation portfolio. The 5-year goals are usually replaced with four or five yearly goals on which the principal is being evaluated. Artifacts and reflections relate directly to these goals and/or to collaboratively developed district leadership criteria or expectations. These artifacts and accompanying reflections are commonly arranged in sections that are representative of the principal's goals or the district leadership criteria or expectations. For example, a principal might divide the artifacts and reflections by goal sections. One principal with whom we worked developed the following goals with her supervisor:

I think that doing my Leadership Framework helped me to really get centered in my beliefs. I wrote it early in September. As I worked toward my goals and district leadership criteria throughout the year, I frequently revisited my framework. I could keep a focus and could tell if decisions being made were in line with it. The reflections I wrote at the end of the year all related to my central beliefs. It was easy to see the connections.

Elementary principal

- To establish a successful testing program so that each child improves on last year's state criterion test scores
- To actively participate in and facilitate the growth of new teachers in the areas of curriculum and student testing
- To create and successfully implement a committee for student management
- To provide parent education evenings where parents can better understand how to help their students to be successful academically

Traditional Evaluation Systems	Evaluation Portfolio Systems
Do not promote professional growth	Promote self-assessment and subsequent growth
Are not perceived to result in significant school improvement	Focus on student achievement and school improvement—this is at the center of all decisions and is reflected in the principal's goals/district criteria
Do not evaluate the substantive aspects of the principal's work	Make professional growth the foundation of the evaluation system; get at what matters for principals to be effective on their respective campuses
Do not address the complexity of the job	Are individualized; take into account all facets of the individual principal's job
Are not authentic; do not afford the opportunity to present concrete evidence of success	Present all successes concretely through authentic artifacts and accompanying reflections
Do not address the contingent and situational aspects of leadership	Allow for the principal to explain decisions, why he or she made the decision, and what the outcomes were
Do not address the moral dimensions of leadership	Keep the values and beliefs of the principal at the core of all decisions made for students and teachers
Do not promote supervisor-principal collaborative relationships	Aid in developing a common set of leadership criteria and goals; are supportive of mentoring relationships
Do not promote ongoing dialogue between or among principals	Promotes dialogue through peer coaching

Figure 4.1. Traditional Evaluation Systems Compared to a System That Includes the Evaluation Portfolio

She divided her portfolio into four sections, one section for each goal, then selected artifacts and developed reflections that related to each of the goals. The supervisor and the principal had agreed earlier on the number of artifacts and the length of the reflections. They had also agreed that the principal would explain in the reflections how her goals related to the campus improvement team's goals and to the district goals.

Figure 4.2 depicts another alternative for organizing the evaluation portfolio. Once areas to be evaluated were agreed on among principals and administrators, the principal sectioned his or her

Administrative Skills	Interpersonal Skills
Seeks new data, new information Interprets data so that it is understandable and usable Uses data for planning and problem solving Identifies resources Secures resources for school improvement efforts Develops a vision that reflects students' needs for academic achievement and success Creates conditions for effective learning to occur	Facilitates groups toward accomplishment of goals Encourages input Coordinates campus improvement efforts Provides support for teachers and parents Coaches other principals Perceives affective needs of others and responds appropriately Motivates self and others
Communication Skills	Knowledge of Self
Effectively communicates verbally and in writing to faculty, staff, parents, and community Makes public professional presentations Keeps faculty informed Makes time to dialogue with faculty	Self-assesses Articulates strengths Minimizes weaknesses Improves weaknesses Continues to learn

Figure 4.2. Sample Criteria Developed for Evaluation Purposes

portfolio accordingly. For example, the four criteria, including performance indicators, were administrative skills, interpersonal skills, communication skills, and knowledge of self. Figure 4.3 on pages 39 and 40 lists artifacts that principals included for documentation for each of the four criteria.

Reflections are central to the evaluation portfolio. They are necessary to describe and reconstruct the artifact that has been selected for inclusion. The reflections follow the reflection cycle featured in Chapter 3 and allow the principal to best represent to the evaluator to what degree he or she has met the established goals or district criteria.

Presenting the Portfolio

The principal will present his or her portfolio to the evaluator(s). An established format, including length of time for the presentation, will be agreed on well in advance of summative evaluation presentations.

Criterion: Administrative Skills	Artifacts
Seeks new data, new information Interprets data so that it is understandable and usable Uses data for planning and problem solving Identifies resources Secures resources for school improvement efforts Develops a vision that reflects students' needs for academic achievement and success Creates conditions for effective learning to occur	*Following are work samples that could be used to demonstrate some of the accompanying criterion indicators:* Copy of a report related to the performance of a group of students including an analysis and interpretation of data Campus improvement goals, revision, and evidence of accomplishment Mini-case study regarding a concern on the campus, including a study of the issue, the steps to solution, and the movement toward results
Criterion: Interpersonal Skills	Artifacts
Facilitates groups toward accomplishment of goals Encourages input Coordinates campus improvement efforts Provides support for teachers and parents Coaches other principals Perceives affective needs of others and responds appropriately Motivates self and others	*Following are work samples that could be used to demonstrate some of the accompanying criterion indicators:* Videotape of the administrator leading a group session or an evaluation from a third party on how the administrator facilitates the group Letters from others expressing appreciation for efforts and initiative Needs assessment of teacher and staff morale along with subsequent action plan Copy of personal/professional goals and evidence of accomplishment Videotape of a conference with a mentee or beginning teacher Collaboratively developed plan for growth of the mentee or beginning teacher *(continued)*

Figure 4.3. Suggested Artifacts for Administrative Portfolio Evaluation

Generally, a presentation will last no more than 30 minutes, including time for clarification and summarization of all points.

The principal should have received the standards by which he or she will be evaluated prior to the beginning of the district

Criterion: Communication Skills	Artifacts
Effectively communicates verbally and in writing to faculty, staff, parents, and community Makes public professional presentations Keeps faculty informed Makes time to dialogue with faculty	*Following are work samples that could be used to demonstrate some of the accompanying criterion indicators:* Copies of newsletters, memoranda, news releases, letters, grants, etc. Evaluations by teachers of faculty meetings or staff development presentations
Criterion: Knowledge of Self	Artifacts
Self-assesses Articulates strengths Minimizes weaknesses Improves weaknesses Continues to learn	*Following are work samples that could be used to demonstrate some of the accompanying criterion indicators:* List of specific ways feedback on performance is gathered Candid reflections on selected experiences or activities and subsequent action plans based on feedback from others, for example, from parents regarding how well a parent conference was conducted Listings, agendas, certificates from workshops, or notes from inquiry group meetings or conferences attended for professional growth Leadership Framework including the discussion of such issues as preferred organizational hierarchy, process for conflict resolution, and maintenance of teacher morale

Figure 4.3. Suggested Artifacts for Administrative Portfolio Evaluation, Continued

evaluation cycle, which usually begins with the development of yearly goals with the supervisor. The evaluation scale or rubric should be directly connected to district criteria. For example, a principal goal to develop a shared mission or vision would be tied to the established district criteria, Administrative Skills. A sample district rubric for the specific criteria, Administrative Skills, is depicted in Figure 4.4. This sample rubric contains three levels by which

---

Level 1 (needs improvement)

    The principal

        Develops a mission for the school

        Minimally assesses the school's instructional configurations

        Shows few indications of changes that are directed to meeting individual needs

        Is intolerant of change

        Shows limited evidence of involving others in the overall operation of the school

        Ineffectively aligns resources to promote student learning

Level 2 (meets expectations)

    The principal

        Develops and facilitates a vision with input from staff, parents, students, and the community to accomplish the school mission

        Designs programs to enhance school improvement efforts

        Supports change efforts on the campus

        Encourages others to become risk takers and stakeholders in the school's improvement efforts

Level 3 (exceeds expectations)

    The principal

        Develops and facilitates the realization of a shared vision that involves staff, parents, students, and the community in the identification and accomplishment of the school's mission

        Acknowledges the individual needs of all staff and students, including those at risk, through exploration, assessment, development, and implementation of effective educational programs

        Encourages and manages constructive change that leads to student achievement

        Encourages and develops the leadership of others in a way that empowers them to become risk takers and stakeholders in the school's improvements efforts

---

Figure 4.4. Sample Rubric for Administrative Skills

a principal's actions depicted in his or her evaluation portfolio would be judged. Rubrics are highly individualized because they are developed by administrators in their respective districts and are reflective of the district's collaboratively developed criteria for leadership. Rubrics may vary from three to six evaluative levels.

    There are two stages in the presentation of the evaluation portfolio: Stage 1,

---

The inclusion of an evaluation portfolio in our evaluation system has been an empowering tool for our principals.

Superintendent

I was nervous when I had to meet with Mr. B. to discuss my portfolio, but he made me feel at ease and urged me to share freely. As I shared, he asked questions about the points I was making. This was a very positive experience for me. In fact, it was the best summative conference I've had.

Assistant principal

prior to the presentation, and Stage 2, the presentation. Prior to presenting the portfolio at the summative conference, Stage 1, the principal will need to ensure that the portfolio is complete and makes a professional impression. The principal will need to prepare transparencies to demonstrate major points or emphasize certain items that are included in the portfolio. In the evaluation portfolio presentation, unlike traditional evaluation systems, the principal is a key player. He or she will focus on, share strengths of, and articulate future plans for improvement that have been determined through the reflections. The principal will want to think about the mentoring and peer coaching experiences he or she has had during the year and be prepared to discuss the effects of those relationships on the principal's improved practice. Finally, it will be beneficial to consider potential questions the evaluator(s) might have, along with possible responses.

Stage 2 is the presentation at the summative conference. The first thing we suggest is to relax and remember to take cues from the evaluator(s). The principal will need to make the presentation uniquely his or hers. Usually, principals share their goals and explain specifically how they met them, explain in what particular areas they feel they have grown professionally, and outline specific skills or projects on which they wish to work and plans for further improvement. At the conclusion of the presentation, the principal should ask for suggestions or if there is any clarification or additional documentation needed to support the claims represented in the portfolio.

Use of the evaluation portfolio creates ownership in the evaluation system and empowers principals to document the complexities, contingencies, and individuality of effective leadership. As the principal examines his or her ability to solve problems or perform tasks in authentic environments, the principal is able to demonstrate graphically those abilities in relation to district criteria for improved practice and increased student achievement.

5

The Principal Portfolio for Career Advancement

I have interviewed assistant principals who have used the portfolio in their interviews. Clearly, they come across as very confident and prepared. I believe the portfolio is a tool that can provide the candidate with a powerful personal image.

Elementary principal

The previous chapters have emphasized the benefits that principals can gain from portfolio development with regard to personal and professional improvement through assessment and evaluation. In this final chapter, we discuss an additional benefit of the principal portfolio. Specifically, this chapter explains the characteristics of the career advancement portfolio, presents advantages of the portfolio for career advancement, describes the contents of the career advancement portfolio, and suggests how it may be included in the interview process.

The Career Advancement Portfolio

The two types of portfolios discussed in previous chapters focus on professional development or evaluation of the principal. The career advancement portfolio differs from these portfolios. It highlights strengths and accomplishments and serves as a reflective and predictive indicator of the potential of the administrative candidate. It is important to keep in mind that this portfolio must be prepared and presented with the ultimate goal of marketing oneself as the most viable candidate for a particular position.

A thoughtful, well-organized portfolio gives interviewers important information about the candidate's leadership strengths, professional values and ethics, problem-solving ability, organizational and communication ability, and objectivity regarding self that might not otherwise be revealed in an interview situation.

This is the best thing I could have done for myself. It really made me see all the things related to leadership I had done in my career.

High school principal

Advantages of the Career Advancement Portfolio

Professionals in the arts and communications industries have traditionally used portfolios to market themselves. This concept has spread to the field of education. For example, Guaglianone (1996) states that "teachers have gained employment by presenting a portfolio at a job interview to demonstrate professional competence, creativity, organization, and skill" (p. 232). Seldin and associates (1993) report that some colleges and universities are using portfolios in the hiring of professors. In our work with administrators, we have found the career advancement portfolio to be of tremendous assistance. Job applicants who have used the career advancement portfolio in the application process, as well as those who have interviewed the applicants, laud the effectiveness of the career advancement portfolio (Brown, Irby, & Shearer, 1996). Figure 5.1 presents representative comments of principal candidates and interviewers regarding the portfolio's importance in job acquisition.

Comments from administrative candidates using the portfolio

When I had my portfolio in the interview, I could readily recall activities I'd participated in.
The portfolio gives physical evidence of my talents; it showcases my abilities.
My portfolio got my foot in the door; I was immediately sent an application.
People said my portfolio gave me a more professional image; made a professional impression.
It gave me a more holistic view of my leadership skills and career.
I felt confident going into the interview; I was better able to articulate my philosophy and to recall immediately specific examples for some of the questions that were asked.

Comments from interviewers

The candidates with the portfolios appeared more confident and more ready to respond.
The applicant who had the portfolio was easier to remember after the interview session; she had used the portfolio briefly during the interview and left it with us.
We were able to see areas of strength before the candidate arrived; it gave us a better picture of this person . . . more than just the application and résumé . . . to tell whether the person was an immediate fit for our district.

Figure 5.1. Comments About the Portfolio From Candidates and Interviewers

Additionally, in leadership courses and seminars that we conduct, participants consistently rate the development of the career advancement portfolio as a highly beneficial and relevant activity (Irby, Brown, & Zunker, 1996) in two significant ways: (a) It assists in building self-confidence prior to going in for an interview for an administrative position, and (b) it demonstrates to the participants the areas in which they need expanded experiences for a particular position, enabling them to recognize "gaps" and aiding in targeting growth areas for goal setting. They also indicate that the career advancement portfolio would give them an important advantage in an interview. They feel more confident to expound on their strengths, minimize their weaknesses, and be assertive in a job interview by presenting a thoughtful plan of remedial action and future development.

Because of competition for administrative positions, serious applicants must set themselves apart from the crowd and must present their credentials in the most positive manner possible. It can no longer be assumed that qualifications and accomplishments simply presented verbally in an interview will be enough to get a job.

The career advancement portfolio offers an authentic and graphic representation that gives a principal an edge in the interview competition. The administrators who have interviewed candidates using the career advancement portfolio have indicated several benefits of the portfolio: (a) Those candidates stand out from the others and come to mind more easily after all interviews are conducted, (b) the information presented in the portfolio provides significant information about the candidate that otherwise would not be provided, and (c) the portfolio gives insights into the applicant that provide a closer opportunity to determine if the applicant will fit well into the campus team, culture, and community.

Contents of the Career Advancement Portfolio

The process of development of the career advancement portfolio, as well as the content and format, is similar to that of the other two types of portfolios. However, because the primary purpose differs, artifacts and accompanying reflections may vary from the professional development portfolio or the evaluation portfolio.

All four of the components of the principal portfolio discussed in Chapter 2 are included in the career advancement portfolio. The first three components of the career advancement portfolio—résumé, Leadership Framework, and 5-year administrative goals—are similar to those already discussed. However, components will be targeted to the position being sought, particularly, the résumé and the goal sections.

The fourth component, artifacts and reflections, will also differ in this type of portfolio in that it will focus on leadership qualities, experiences, and accomplishments that are related to the position sought. The artifacts might be arranged in sections that are representative of the particular job description. Figure 5.2 shows the following sections that have proven to be reflective of most administrative positions, along with examples of artifacts:

Leadership experiences. In this section the administrator will want to select artifacts that reflect various aspects of leadership such as vision, problem solving, organizational skills, planning and goal-setting skills, and management abilities.

Curriculum and instruction experiences. This section should document the administrator's ability to facilitate the development and revision of curriculum, assessment of student and teacher growth related to curriculum and instruction, evaluation or assessment of programs, awareness of current trends and best practices in curriculum and instruction, or other related issues.

Student, parent, and community interactions. In this section, administrators will share how they have facilitated collaboration between or among groups within or outside the school, how they have gathered feedback from those particular groups and used the feedback for improvement, or how they have developed partnerships with organizations or institutions in the school area.

Presentations and committees. This section should address presentations given by the administrator to professional or civic organizations, community groups, faculty, or teachers and should offer evidence of the ability to work well with others in the accomplishment of goals. These artifacts illustrate effective communication with groups as well as the professional image portrayed to those groups. Additionally, the administrator should address in this section participation on local, state, regional, or national committees that demonstrates commitment to education and to the community.

Professional growth, staff development experiences, and training. Evidence in this section should portray the administrator as a continuous, life-long learner by providing examples of participation in professional growth opportunities. Additionally, the principal should include documents related to his or her ability to ascertain professional growth needs of others and to develop and plan programs to address those needs.

Performance evaluations. Some administrators include a section on prior performance evaluations. They place an appraisal form with scores or a formal evaluation letter from the supervisor in this section.

Accolades. This section offers an opportunity for the administrator to demonstrate his or her credibility among colleagues, students, par-

Section	Suggested Artifacts
Leadership experiences	Mini-case study regarding a concern on the campus (e.g., gang-related activity) including a study of the issue, the steps to solution, and the movement toward results
Curriculum and instruction experiences	A copy of a plan for the revision of curriculum that includes integrated curriculum An executive brief describing the status of students and teachers on the campus in terms of growth during a 3-year period
Student, parent, and community interactions	An agenda of a meeting of a combined group of individuals working on a campus project in a collaborative manner A brief portion of a video of the administrator conducting a collaborative meeting
Presentations and committees	A letter of invitation to serve on a national committee or a copy of pages from a conference brochure that indicates the administrator's name on that committee A cover page of the handout packet used in a presentation by the administrator A product of committee work (e.g., a handbook, bylaws, strategic plan)
Professional growth, staff development experiences, and training	Programs, agendas, or certificates from workshops attended A needs assessment of teachers and a subsequent action plan for staff development
Performance evaluations	Completed appraisal or evaluation form
Accolades	Newspaper articles about the campus Letters from parents or colleagues Certificates of honors

Figure 5.2. Career Advancement Portfolio Sections With Suggested Artifacts

ents, or the community and should include documentation of hon-
ors, awards, support, or commendation.

Figure 5.3 presents an actual artifact with a reflection from a career advancement portfolio. As is the case with the other types of portfolios, the reflections that accompany the artifact are of utmost importance. In these reflections applicants have the opportunity to really "sell" the reviewer on their competencies, accomplishments, and attitudes. It is through the reflections that candidates are able to convey to employers the substance of who they really are and what their personal value systems, growth, and visions are.

I decided to put a vita at the end of my portfolio rather at the beginning because it was too long. I knew the reader would not want to look at it immediately. I tried to sell the reader first and entice him or her into reading the longer vita. I talked to the reader (my principal) later, and it worked!

Assistant principal

Presenting the Portfolio

Administrators and prospective administrators who have used the portfolio in the interview process have presented the portfolio in a variety of ways. Their experiences have yielded several options for when and how to present the portfolio:

1. *Submission with the application:* Some applicants have submitted their portfolios at the same time that they have submitted the required materials for application for the position. Several indicate that voluntarily submitting their portfolio has been of tremendous benefit in getting them an interview; interviewers concur.

2. *Submission in advance:* Frequently, applicants have been requested to submit the portfolio in advance of the interview so that the interviewer or the interview team may have a more complete picture of the applicant's experiences and expertise prior to the interview. Interviewers explain that reviewing the portfolio in advance assists in designing appropriate questions for individuals. Additionally, this preview allows the interview team to begin to assess the match between the applicant's philosophy and skills and the school's expectations and needs.

Criteria:	Leadership
Goal:	To develop a shared vision or mission for the campus
Artifact:	An agenda from a meeting with staff
	An agenda from a meeting with parents
	An agenda from a meeting with students
	The mission of the school

These artifacts are important documents that demonstrate my ability to lead a group toward a shared mission and vision for the school. I selected 20 individuals from each group, randomly, to meet in three separate meetings to seek their input for the development of the school's mission. We met during the months of September and October. As the reader can see the first three artifacts led up to the fourth artifact, which is the mission. Through this process other areas of need for the campus (or areas of change) were identified. The mission directs us in a path of change and we have already begun to develop an action plan for those changes. We developed a campus team that includes four parents, four teachers, and two students, who are working on the action plan. Items addressed in the action plan that grew out of the new mission are: student motivation, parent involvement, staff development on improving test scores, and gang involvement prevention. Additionally, the action plan includes more involvement activities for the community and for parents and teachers to develop subplans for improvements on the campus. I am supportive of these changes and have redirected some of the budget in staff development to substitutes for teachers who need to be freed for the planning days. This is the year for planning all strategies and beginning staff and parental development series. Next year all action plans will be in effect.

Figure 5.3. Sample Artifact and Reflection for Career Advancement

3. *Unsolicited submission at the interview:* Applicants have also taken their portfolios unsolicited to the interview. Several interview teams have requested that the portfolio be passed around during the interview so that interviewers might ask clarifying or probing questions.

4. *Presentation at the interview:* A few applicants report that they have made a brief, formal presentation of their portfolio's contents at the beginning of the interview as they introduced themselves to the team or to the individual interviewer. Some interviewers point out that one has to be cautious with this approach because of the time constraints in an interview setting. Although suggesting that on some occasions it may be possible to schedule in advance the time for a brief overview of the portfolio, interviewers indicate that even this "scheduled portfolio time" would be limited to 5 to 10 minutes.

5. *Example during the interview:* Other applicants have used the portfolio during the interview but have not made a presentation or passed the portfolio around. Keeping the portfolio themselves, they have pointed out particular examples or artifacts to enhance an answer to a specific question. For example, when one applicant was asked about her experience in planning, designing, and conducting staff development activities, she opened her portfolio to the staff development section, which contained several staff development agendas as well as workshop participant evaluation summaries. Not only was she able to elaborate on the answer, she was also able to discuss a specific workshop that she knew was needed on that particular campus, quickly and easily providing concrete examples of her success.

6. *Leave with the interview team:* Some of the applicants report that they have briefly referred to their portfolio during the interview, but rather than presenting it or pointing out specific examples, they have simply left it for later review by the interviewer(s). This approach has also yielded positive benefits. Candidates state that going by later to pick up their portfolio provided them an opportunity for a follow-up visit with the interviewer or the head of the interview team. All report that the interviewer made positive comments or asked additional questions after having reviewed the portfolio.

Above, we have listed six possibilities for using the portfolio in conjunction with interviews; other options may exist. Two cautions are in order. First, regardless of the option selected, it is important that the candidate not be overbearing or intrusive in the sharing of the portfolio. Applicants must be sensitive to the norms and expectations of the particular campus or district interview process. As in any interview, the candidate must be able to "read" the interviewer(s)

I had a colleague of mine, actually she was like a peer coach, look at my portfolio before I went for the interview. I wanted to make sure I had highlighted all my accomplishments and presented them in a way that was easy to understand. Also I wanted her to see if my reflections were the best they could be and that they were effective analyses of my professional growth in leadership. I think a peer coach reviewing the portfolio is good idea; they know your work and can help showcase that work.

Assistant principal

When I interviewed, I left the portfolio with the assistant superintendent. That allowed me to make an appearance a few days later to pick it up. (Not out of sight, not out of mind!)

Junior high principal

---

and respond appropriately. Second, it is important to note that district and campus procedures for the interview vary; the applicant should endeavor to ascertain in advance the appropriate time for sharing the portfolio.

The career advancement portfolio is an effective tool for pursuing positions, seeking promotions, and assessing applicants. Artifacts and accompanying reflections represent the candidate's strengths and accomplishments that might not otherwise be apparent in the typical résumé or interview, and they reveal information about the individual's organizational and communication skills, philosophy, capacity for leadership and vision, commitment to professional growth, ability to anticipate problems and develop alternatives, risk-taking behavior, and willingness to accept challenging assignments.

Resource A:
Commonly Asked Questions
About the Use of Portfolios

Are portfolios worth the time and effort?

It is true that portfolio development takes time. Time is required for the actual compilation of the portfolio as well as for the completion of the reflection cycle (see Chapter 3). Principals report that once artifacts have been selected to be included, the portfolio can be completed in about 8 to 10 hours. According to principals, assistant principals, and aspiring administrators with whom we have worked, the portfolio is well worth the time and effort. They point out that developing the portfolios improves their self-confidence and enhances their abilities to reflect on strengths while planning for the correction of weaknesses. Other benefits cited are that portfolios provide visible evidence of the administrator's accomplishments, which may otherwise go unnoticed by the supervising administrator or an interview team, give evaluators an insightful glimpse into what the principal has done to solve problems, and allow them to plan for the accomplishment of goals.

Does the development of a portfolio really improve principal performance?

The literature is replete with supportive reports of improved teaching and learning by teachers and students who use portfolios. We have found that when principals use portfolios, their performance also improves. Portfolios assist principals in reflecting on their experiences, setting goals, developing plans for reaching those goals, and determining if their practices have improved through the process of goal attainment. Particularly in the case of the evaluation portfolio, the principal is able to determine mastery or nonmastery of district-developed leadership standards or proficiencies. Additionally, the evaluation portfolio offers a valuable tool for professional feedback in formative and summative evaluations. Physical evidence in the form of artifacts and reflections is available to facilitate dialogue between the principal and the supervising administrator, as well as among principals who may be in peer coaching situations. In the final analysis, of course, it is the individual principal who determines the extent of improvement that results from the portfolio process.

Isn't portfolio evaluation too subjective?

Maintaining objectivity in any personnel evaluation system is always a challenge. As with other evaluation systems, it is very important to remove as much subjectivity as possible. To do so, district personnel need to (a) establish district standards, competencies, or proficiencies for leadership and ensure that these standards are clearly communicated to all involved; (b) develop and disseminate a rubric for scoring the portfolio (a rubric is a 3- to 6-point scale designed to evaluate demonstrated performance of specific competencies); (c) make certain that the rubric has sufficient detail so that all administrators are clear regarding what represents mastery or nonmastery of the various standards or competencies; and (d) provide thorough training in the use of the rubric to all appraisers. In addition, all district personnel must realize that the administrator's evaluation must focus on his or her ability to analyze or interpret the problem or situation, select and use appropriate strategies to solve the problem or address the situation, appropriately connect leadership experiences to district standards, and ultimately improve practice.

Because personnel decisions will result from the use of the evaluation portfolio, it is subject to more exact and intense scrutiny than the portfolio that has as its sole purpose professional growth. In developing an evaluation system inclusive of a portfolio, it is helpful to have a knowledgeable and experienced consultant to guide the district personnel through the process. The consultant needs to be competent in general administrative evaluation systems as well as in all aspects of the portfolio evaluation system, including the development of portfolios, reflections, and standards and rubrics. In addition, the consultant must have expertise in the scoring of portfolios, group facilitation, conferencing, and coaching.

Is it the attractive, impressive, well-written portfolio that results in the highest evaluation?

No. Of course, the portfolio should be professional in appearance, but an attractive portfolio is no disguise for weak leadership. The portfolio should be evaluated on established leadership standards and predeveloped rubrics. The evaluation of the writing itself is not the key issue; rather, it is the evaluation of the substance and impact of the leadership experiences. The evaluation should focus on the principal's abilities to identify and solve problems and plan for improved schooling. The artifacts should substantiate the abilities proclaimed in the portfolio. Evidence of effective leadership based on established criteria must be apparent to the reviewers for high evaluations to occur. Training for reviewers or evaluators is an important aspect in the use of evaluation portfolios. It is critical that reviewers and all concerned agree on what demonstrates mastery and how to appropriately use the rubric; therefore, interrater reliability using the developed rubrics must be established.

Why would an evaluation portfolio include the Leadership Framework?

The Leadership Framework is a summarization of the primary beliefs and attitudes of the administrator regarding leadership (see Chapter 2). The creation of the framework should be the first written reflection for the portfolio. It provides a foundation for all other reflections on experiences. The writing of the Leadership Framework compels principals to reflect on their philosophy of leadership, learning, and teaching. It allows principals to assess their beliefs as those beliefs relate to the district's expectations and allows the supervising administrator the opportunity to assess whether the district's expectations match the principal's. These are important factors in the principal's satisfaction with his or her position within a specific school district and with his or her "fit" in the district.

References

Athanases, S. Z. (1994). Teachers' reports on the effects of preparing portfolios of literacy instruction. *The School Journal, 94,* 421-439.

Brogan, B. R. (1995). *The case for teacher portfolios.* Paper presented at the 47th annual meeting of the American Association of Colleges for Teacher Education, Washington, DC. (ERIC Document Reproduction Service No. ED 381 516)

Brown, G., & Irby, B. J. (1996a). [The administrative portfolio evaluation system]. Unpublished raw data.

Brown, G., & Irby, B. J. (1996b). *The Administrative Portfolio Evaluation System Institute manual.* Huntsville, TX: Sam Houston State University Press.

Brown, G., Irby, B. J., & Chance, J. W. (1996). Reflective Performance Scale. In *Administrative Portfolio Evaluation System Institute manual.* Huntsville, TX: Sam Houston State University Press.

Brown, G., Irby, B. J., Garrison, L., Shearer, S., & Smith, S. (1996). *Helpful hints for using the portfolio.* Paper presented at the Women in Educational Leadership seminar, Huntsville, TX.

Brown, G., Irby, B. J., & Shearer, S. (1996). [Qualitative study on the use of administrative portfolios]. Unpublished raw data.

Bull, K. S., Montgomery, D., Coombs, L., Sebastian, J., & Fletcher, R. (1994). *Portfolio assessment in teacher evaluation: A comparison of the perspectives of general and special education administrators and teachers.* (ERIC Document Reproduction Service No. ED 369 604)

Buschman, L. (1993, January). Portfolios: Windows on learning. *Learning 93*, pp. 22-25.

DePree, K. R. (1974, February). *Administration evaluation: Problems, process and strategies.* Paper presented at the annual convention of the American Association of School Administrators, Atlantic City, NJ.

Doolittle, P. (1994). *Teacher portfolio assessment.* (ERIC Document Reproduction Service No. ED 385 608)

Drake, T. L., & Roe, W. H. (1994). *The principalship* (4th ed.). New York: Macmillan.

Grant, C. A., & Zeichner, K. M. (1984). On becoming a reflective teacher. In C. A. Grant (Ed.), *Preparing for reflective teaching* (pp. 1-18). Boston: Allyn & Bacon.

Guaglianone, C. L. (1996). *Portfolio assessment of administrators. Prioritizing instruction, the fourth yearbook of the National Council of Professors of Educational Administration.* Lancaster, PA: Technomic.

Harrison, W. C., & Peterson, K. D. (1986). *Pitfalls in the evaluation of principals.* Paper presented at the 67th annual meeting of the American Educational Research Association, San Francisco. (ERIC Document Reproduction Service No. ED 277 131)

Hoy, W. K., & Miskel, C. G. (1987). *Leadership in educational administration: Theory, research and practice.* New York: Random House.

Irby, B. J., Brown, G., & Zunker, W. (1996, July). *A program evaluation seminar for women in educational leadership.* Presentation at Women Leading: Bridges to the Future, annual conference of the Texas Council of Women School Executives, Austin.

Joyce, B., & Showers, B. (1995). *Student achievement through staff development* (2nd ed.). White Plains, NY: Longman.

Kroeze, D. J. (1984). Effective principals as instructional leaders: New directions for research. *Administrator's Notebook, 30*(9), 1-4.

Leithwood, K. A. (1987). Using the principal profile to assess performance. *Educational Leadership, 45*(1), 63-66.

Leithwood, K. A., & Stager, M. (1986, April). *Differences in problem-solving processes used by moderately and highly effective principals.* Paper presented at the annual meeting of the American Educational Research Association, San Francisco.

Lewis, A. C. (1982). The principal's role: Evaluating the evaluator. In *Evaluating educational personnel* (pp. 73-78). Arlington, VA: American Association of School Administrators. (ERIC Document Reproduction Service No. ED 212 055)

Lindahl, R. A. (1987). Evaluating the principal's performance: An essential step in promoting school excellence. *Education, 108,* 204-211.

Pellicer, L. O., Anderson, L. W., Keefe, J. W., Kelly, E. A., & McCleary, L. E. (1988). *High school leaders and their schools: Vol. 1. A national profile.* Reston, VA: National Association of Secondary School Principals.

Redfern, G. B. (1972). Principals: Who's evaluating them, why, and how? *NASSP Bulletin, 56*(34), 85-93.

Redfern, G. B. (1980). *Evaluating teachers and administrators: A performance objective approach.* Boulder, CO: Westview.

Roe, M. F. (1991). *Portfolios: From mandate to implementation.* Paper presented at the 41st annual meeting of the National Reading Conference, Palm Springs, CA. (ERIC Document Reproduction Service No. ED 343 103)

Schon, D. A. (1993). *The reflective practitioner.* New York: Basic Books.

Scriven, M. (1988). *Evaluating teachers as professionals.* (ERIC Document Reproduction Service No. ED 300 882)

Seldin, P., & Associates. (1993). *Successful use of teaching portfolios.* Boston, MA: Anker.

Sergiovanni, T., & Starratt, R. J. (1988). *Supervision: Human perspectives* (4th ed.). New York: McGraw-Hill.

Shoemaker, J., & Fraser, H. W. (1981). What principals can do: Some implications from studies of effective schooling. *Phi Delta Kappan, 63,* 178-182.

Sweeney, J. (1982). Research synthesis on effective school leadership. *Educational Leadership, 39,* 346-352.

Tierney, D. S. (1993). *Teaching portfolios: 1992 update on research and practice.* (ERIC Document Reproduction Service No. ED 361 357)

Vizyak, L. (1994). Student portfolios: Building self-reflection in a first-grade classroom. *The Reading Teacher, 48,* 362-367.

Walker, D. (1971). A naturalistic model for curriculum development. *School Review, 80*(1).

CORWIN
PRESS

The Corwin Press logo—a raven striding across an open book—represents the happy union of courage and learning. We are a professional-level publisher of books and journals for K-12 educators, and we are committed to creating and providing resources that embody these qualities. Corwin's motto is "Success for All Learners."